Turbulence in Small Spaces

poems by

Adele Evershed

Finishing Line Press
Georgetown, Kentucky

Turbulence in Small Spaces

Copyright © 2023 by Adele Evershed
ISBN 979-8-88838-301-8 First Edition
All rights reserved under International and Pan-American Copyright Conventions. No part of this book may be reproduced in any manner whatsoever without written permission from the publisher, except in the case of brief quotations embodied in critical articles and reviews.

Publisher: Leah Huete de Maines
Editor: Christen Kincaid
Cover Art: *Busy Days* by Catrin Welz-Stein
Author Photo: Joseph DeRuvo
Cover Design: Elizabeth Maines McCleavy

Order online: www.finishinglinepress.com
also available on amazon.com

Author inquiries and mail orders:
Finishing Line Press
PO Box 1626
Georgetown, Kentucky 40324
USA

Table of Contents

Skewwhiff 1

Gifts to a Young Lady 2

A Guide to Flash-In-The-Pan Living 3

Daisy In Chains 4

Illusions Of a Starry Knight 5

Watching Dr. Zhivago with My Sister 6

Splash-A Retrospective 7

Lines 8

The Fibs We Tell 9

Maybe I Give a Damn 10

A Romance Without Comedy 11

Mulling Over First Love 12

Interdependence 13

Air Turbulence in Small Spaces 14

Choosing Chocolates in A Pandemic 15

Passive: Aggressive 16

Relax—Don't Do It 17

Beyond the Belief of Selkies 18

brink 20

Brown Rapping 21

March 22

Let's Have a Jar 23

after the storm
I stand in the rain shadow
blurred at the edges...

For Nick, Megan, Owen, Rhys and Dylan who continue to help me weather the storm

Skewwhiff

I woke up yellow—decrepit—something not quite right
People born by the sea are older—yet this weathering surprised me

The compression of the thing settled in my gut
Rigmaroling me round the room like a drunk—yet I still couldn't fill up the empty spaces

Time once felt slippery in patches—skidding past—a flibberty-jibbit
Now it just hangs like a promise—each day a small fable

I dig out abeyant words—yet use them in all the wrong places
Washing them with my breath—so they can exist for a short time

Capering about they create their own mild breeze
—amorphous
—they float away on a riptide and I am too gutless to call them back

Gifts To a Young Lady

in the bathroom you with your cracked skin (call it marbling) and pulsating mound are offered gifts that you bundle in hands and mouths to taunt the brittle beauty promised but better down the stairs the stuffing of apples into pink plastic so with the grace of tearing out comes a reliquary smell found in forgotten books and ruddy leaf piles moldering rusty cumbersomely heavy as you crunch bird bones beneath a white robe to hide from the divine—too divine—breaking a witch-hazel rod you secretly divine a sewer to baptize and generously mold wild things to make a wooden bowl where you can stack the bruised apples before the fall and know that nobody no matter how lovely ever had all the answers

A Guide to Flash-In-The-Pan Living

They told you / don't want more / hide the teeth of your tongue / show the veins in your wrists / flashy and vulnerable as those on a cow's udder / powder the cleft of you / make a beckoning bowl with your hands / suck your hair like a gag / hope that is enough

But later you lay the drunken rib of the stuff / calling in the yellow light / you feel the dragging length of them / overwintered lumpen / large / flightless / fightless / talking about beautiful things as if they were ugly / so you leave behind your urine town / practice turning people into hills / freely look back / not minding the turnings / tell old stories / order coffee with foam / pretend all incidental noise is the sound of angels' wings / scrunch up so your edges meet / lay eggs like a magpie / nest in others' pulls and snags / take the slinken things / wrap them fast in a fever amulet / tie it round your neck / tell yourself they're safe / and only things in pouches scream

You tell them / they always deserve more / not to listen if they say you cannot be an X / always, always, always, show your teeth / when things make you smile / and especially when they don't / flick your hair like freedom / and they will always be enough

It does not matter if you drown in the middle of the sea or close to sure—you are still dead—so don't let the only fascinating thing be— you've gone

Daisy in Chains

My pale head hovers above the wrinkled pillow of my cheeks
—signaling I should not drown today
but so—I'm shackled tacitly to this vulgar time of bedding
a day's eye might see the sorrow and stoop—
remembering how I was told to hide my shiny places
and not speak of tempting sunny day stuff

Pile stones around the hawthorn to stop the cows from coming

I ignored the ladling hands stripping the pale petals
—their spittled symphonies sound in the underground
because he loves me—he loves me not—
now they are left to crudle in common necks of the wood—
And we keen to reclaim them by candlelight or leave a trail
—of paper doves crying and playing up innocence in fallen feathers
yet still they say—look closely—hairs grow in the cracks
even on the leaf of the loveliest flower

Pile stones around the hawthorn to stop the cows from coming

If we dance like happy Hollyhocks in every summer garden
—as tall as a wish against the violent walls and sermon stones
then all the flitting things can find sanctuary in our green towers
we will swish our mighty purple skirts in a flamenco of tumbling pods
and the seasons will sing—how small is what we know
yet it will be the sweetest story—safely sown by our own hands

Pile the stones around the hawthorn to save the cows from coming

Illusions Of a Starry Knight

your brutal words balance on my arms in stacks of dirty plates
as I pencil trees in what Brock, the art instructor, calls 'Van Gogh style'
not a forest or a wood, not even a copse but a singular black hulk
surrounded by a triangular fence—aloof and as far removed from the
divine as a hotdog

the limbs wave in stabs and snatches—the spiky leaves spiraling cruelly
filling all the space making it difficult to breath
Brock looks over and smiles saying, 'Your tree is fifty shades of grey'
of course he's alluding to that badly edited bestseller—full of
borderline abuse
your abuse is always beautifully polished—never in my face always
just under my skin

my pencil snaps as I grimace at Brock—picking up a bright yellow oil
pastel
I amaze myself and morph the leaves into stars that swirl in the
darkness
dropping my arms the plates smithereen and become just an empty
task for a woman with a broom
And as I pack my bag, somewhere in the divine I feel Van Gogh wink

Watching Dr. Zhivago With My Sister

When I told you there was no poetry in snow
You said it was a space to fill with other stuff—angels and men who could not leave
All the undercover things from our childhood

You played tragedy like a balalaika in your background
Dancing with the snowflake people—babbling they were made up of everything that was not here

You would hold up your hands to nail the stars
Fixing them as a slipped cross so I could find you
After—you put your bloody fingers to my mouth—and this gesture always tasted oh so old

Now the cold scolds my bones choking me from the ground up—
like a snowflake I am made up of what is not there
Still I always look for you in the pinprick light of a cinema or in the chaos of shapes leaving a bus

Even though I know you are spinning rings far away
Beyond the illusion of stars or redemption

Splash-A Retrospective

                                      It was always there—lurking at the edges
          And I wonder if knowing the situation would have been enough
In the movies mermaids are touchingly naïve
A sweet affectation to reel us in
But real women have always worked with fish
Travelling on land to gut herrings
Mending nets in living rooms
And no matter where the work there's always a smell
                    And sometimes the sneaking of the relentless minds
                        That couldn't leap from sitcom to a great idea
                            Brings us a popular movie that stinks
                          And—splash—you fell in love with mermaids
                            The story of being saved from drowning—
                      A metamorphosis from human to something fishy
                            Like walking naked onto Ellis Island
Then you always wanted to grow a tail
But later you loved to show your legs
Shimmering in the waves of wind
Iridescent blues and purples and reds
Hard pretty scales—a mermaid at last
You told me—you'd a shell and all
So you wouldn't end up like me
                                  Instead you went over the wall
                                  Knowing the importance
                              Of looking directly into the camera
                        As you got into the water—without a splash
                          That sweet touch a meaningless rotation

                  That left the page as empty as possible

Lines

  I used to hang our washing on a clothesline,
The towels like bunting—getting in a flap
Then the sun would work its magic and bleach away the dirt of us
But later we bought a dryer so our sheets looked the same
Yet had the tang of something unpleasant

                              I use the lines on my face as a loom—
            Fabricating long strings to tie me to our tragic minutiae
            (Please don't call them wrinkles; call them life lines)
                            I can let you read me—line by line
                              And still I won't make sense to you

                                I used to gnaw at the oblong box—
                              Scared to get out—terrified to stay
                            So each time I moved my red lines
            Until the only place I could find them was on my lips
Scarlet gloss— your pseudo-wife—fault lines covered by powder

You with your basic geometry only saw my angles—
So for old times' sake I hung the washing out again
A good-bye and good riddance flapping on the wire
                                        the end of the line

The Fibs We Tell

Our
love
story
only worked
in imaginings
I stood on the ice pretending
I could not hear the cracking noise
Shouting all my truths
And melting
after
you
left

A
ghost
story
only works
on the radio
when truth depends on sound effects
and in vivid imaginings
dying at the scene
a peaceful
floating
like
ice

An
old
story
can be changed
in the retelling
not too scared to kiss you good-bye
I recast myself as fearless
skating on thin ice
a mind shift
and you
would
stay

Maybe I Give a Damn

I always thought I settled for less—for snatches. That first time when you asked if the devil looked like you, I kissed you as if I was Scarlett O'Hara. I let you think you had the wicked glint of Rhett Butler rather than the dull patina of poor old beige Ashley. It was the start of all my unsaid things.

We both study the decaying leaves trapped in a web outside the kitchen window they tremble like chimes that have lost their music; a clumping cluster in the corner of the pane then they trail off like people leaving a party too soon. I should take a broom to them or try to capture the brittle beauty in a photo—I do neither. You make a comment that it might be time to give the house a general spruce up. It's not much of a conversation starter so I shrug on my coat and head out for a walk.

What does disappointment smell like? Is it the scent of another steak and kidney pie that oozes gravy like a bloody wound, that is pushed around your plate until it disintegrates into mush? I know you don't care for suet crust pastry but I serve it occasionally anyway. I play a little game to see how much of it you will eat. Tonight you surprise me; you eat the whole damn thing. When I look out of the window the leaves and the web are gone.

A Romance Without Comedy

When was the last time you heard something so small
Yet it was able to enlarge your soul?
You could feel the upset of the natural rhythms
Yet you suspected this was not meant for you

We played the same song in our heads
Now we make less and less eye contact
My body misses that elastic time of falling
And just as quickly the words are gone,

These days the sounds are more muted
People do talk about how they dream but not I—
I painstakingly rewind and look at the words
And see that often they were meaningless

Yet I can still catch the important ones like—
Do not break a person

Mulling Over First Love

Dark short inside days served chilled to the bone
—air heavy with cinnamon and citrus

and longing. Running from chapel trailing midwinter carols
—hacked on smoky, white, breath

under a dropped pearl necklace of stars
—that first rough, green, mistletoe kiss

Much later on a colder day as sleet fell like confetti
—laying a cold fleece over everything

I thought I knew. The broken branches clutched decay
—but still managed to wave on high

as I walked away. Instead of blood and bandages
—the snow covered Firethorn tree

makes me think of berries and ice-cream
—and this is how I have survived.

Interdependence

Let's arrange some matters
Feelings beat like an enigma in a pine box—decidedly vulgar on the tip of your tongue
And so you bargain with your loveliness

Intellect you dispose of with freaks of fancy
But the truth is peculiar—capturing a heart with a few words
So you handle with care
Knowing your faulty appreciation of absence can cause you to fall and get lost
Under a full moon—the crowded wreck of you
Cuts away what remained
Making you flat and heavy—to all appearances dead
At some more appropriate time it would be a most lovely death
Instead in disgust—you personate—another pseudo-wife
Hanging a copy of "The Last Supper" in the faint hope of saving yourself
Yet it is a rare thing for you to sleep soundly at night.

Air Turbulence in Small Spaces

I've never been able to whistle, but on the radio, a father and daughter have made whistling their life's work. They are performing the Archers' theme, and they sound so happy. Their hero is Ronnie Ronalde, an artist who blew for Marilyn Monroe and the Queen. There's talk about shepherds and plowboys and music by Bach. Then the presenter plays the last bars of '(Sittin' On) The Dock of the Bay' and says how sad it sounds because Otis Redding recorded it right before he died. But surely everyone knows that's not why it's painful. Suddenly they switch to whistling languages. They call it 'speaking without tongues.' I look over to tell you, "Wouldn't that be an excellent title for a Netflix dystopia limited series?" But, of course, you're not there.

Next, a man with a tambourine voice says, you can whistle with an accent and use whistling speech for poetry and seduction. I think about that Bacall line—put your lips together and blow. Finally, his voice like long sweetening, a different man gives different advice, "Spread your lips wide, smile." But I've forgotten how.

Apparently, pitch always depends on the opening of the lips, so I lick my lips, purse and there's a sound like grief. But it's probably only the wind, and since you've gone, there's nobody to hear me anyway.

Choosing Chocolates in a Pandemic

I watch the eyelid petals of the last poppy—waiting for them to drop
Missing mornings when you would wash me with your breath—
You always offered a different sort of danger—like eating chocolates without reading the list
—never knowing if I would get a caramel or a hard nut to swell my throat shut

Rain falls in threads and I hear the ascending notes of my phone—
my nerves swoop in murmurations to remind me I already know what falling feels like
After—I unwrap your favorite purple one and think about eating it for the longest time
—but I have always done my best to stay away from bridges and other high places

Passive: Aggressive

The sea roses glob up on the foot of the slab
And the driftwood about us has piled in irregular rhythms
Remains of not so ancient quarrels are buried on dirty sighs
We poured ourselves in measures—rationing the twists
But still when we lay down it felt like climbing and we couldn't breathe
Our house confronts the sea—once it was a comfort to battle it together
Still the salt air is a constant foe—sand silts up each opening
So I prize myself out with care—without you
Now knowing what things seem I embed in the crumbling cliffs
An ammonite curled in on myself—elemental
Waiting to be hacked out of the milky slice
And weighed in hands so others can feel the gravity of the thing
They will hang me on a shelf and write out a label or a warning
She never fought back but her substance made others wild—

When I was young I asked my mother why she put up with my father's drinking
She looked stunned—she never knew she had a choice
I still think about this all the time

Relax—Don't Do It

Today a woman went mad in the supermarket / it could have happened anywhere really / the only surprising thing was / it had taken her so long / to despair

she licked her lips by the frozen fish / tasting all the sweat / and tears / and lost oceans / so she became as elemental as the tilt of the earth

unfurling amongst the pots of pears / she was an orphaned negative / grown in Argentina / packed in Thailand / and found on a Sainsbury's shelf in Aberdare

in the concrete car park / all the barren trees / fenced in and wound in fairy lights / twinkled like the dying stars / as she was wound in blankets / and told to just relax

Beyond the Belief of Selkies

Mythology bowdlerizes your background—tales of blood and eggs
and sacrifice
Stone circles grew behind the supermarket and a castle crumbled
down the road laying
trails of knights—and it left you with your instincts inside out

Later you shed your blemished skin and grew rangy limbs, longing
for something you
knew you would never find
And then on a spring tide he was there and you began to doubt
yourself

You were gleeful at the ice cream Sunday service—dressed in vanilla
lace, sprinkles of rice in your hair
Wrapped in a fun fur you thought he'd keep you warm forever— but
he never understood the negative space of you—

So he burnt your skin and called it love
And you left as fast as your long legs would carry you—striding in
land where there was
no magic or salt in the air—a place where your seal-song was like the
moaning of the wind

Now you are old and bloodless and flushed, washed back to the shore
to marvel at the
ongoingness of the tide
And the benches telling a whole life in a few words—each one
sounding too much the same—
yet able to make one heart smile

You buy your own bench and sit alongside the wavering sea so much
like yourself—
leaving and coming back again
You've cut words to show you can be grey and beautiful. Alone and
happy

Yet at the end you can still sense the tang of that ancient longing—
that unforgivable
thing that forced you to hide your true self
Just for the feeling of someone else's tongue in your mouth

brink

The corpse bird waits for the last leaf
I once could stroll home no matter the hour
Now my asking sounds like begging
And I am worse off than a widower
As your corpse is still here to remind me
I try to stretch resolve and splinter clouds
But my body is lumpy—like a badger in a bag
Instead I make lists of favorite foods
—last comfort to be served by the woman in white
It is what it isn't—part of a thing I know now
Like taking you to Starbucks because I didn't know your name
I remember instead when the boats delivered milk and butter
Mam making pancakes as thick as her stockings
And the skipping forecast rattling through the radio
Sheep in the meadow, cows in the corn…..
What was the month that I was born?
The cat layered on my lap like a gravity blanket
Her indifference has the insistence of arthritis
I think I am a dog person—you say no
I am bothered by your smell—sweet like subterfuge
'No pissing in the alley' you shout, but I'm desperate
Am I waning? Waning after waxing. Mooning as I piss
All things bright and gone

When I fall I try not to scream and disturb the robin
That death bird might take my corpse
And refashion it into a rope as round as a puddle
Don't grieve—you can't weep for someone you never knew
Tell it all to the paper doves or the last poppies
Petals like eyelids, seeds like black holes—gone in a blink
I wonder—am I going to heaven or hell or to the Vegan Kitchen?
I think I eat bacon—a woman who says her name is Ruth says not
As she spoons bile between my lips or maybe it is just Jell-O

Brown Rapping

Once I was so full up with what I thought I knew—an egg tipped on the floor will burst—unless you boil it—hard—and then it just cleaves—a mosaic of unreliable parts—like a book that has lost its binding

My mother poured tea with the weight of her stories in that sea-kelped town of glam—borrowing portions of other plots—the veins in her wrists—like the underside of a leaf—always led back to where we started—her body a cabinet of curiosity—the stuffed fish of her cheeks—the binary code between her eyebrows—her map of wrinkles—the moon tracks lumbering lightly over her belly where things sparked wonder.

Later—when I came to understand patience—practicing turning people into hotels—hefting my reliquary of decay beneath my clothes—fucking partly dressed or wrapped in pitch—reeking of haphazard crises and splurged sheets—I could put out fires with my piss—feel the pressure of childbirth in my defecations—but then the world fell through me—sprawling on a garage forecourt so flat I could step in it.

How small it is—what I know now—the beetles of the night pipe crowd sounds—the weight of all my deeds dribble down my leg—lounging like spilt tea—leaving behind dirty brown rings of blah—if I bind myself in paper will that stop me disappearing?

March

When you wished to be a better poet you made up words
Cutting through rejections like a sacred cow
Now your dead outnumber the living
And tears fill the vase of you

In your shed sprays of daffodils name the light—glowery
And Armstrong's trumpet names the noise—a perfect din
But they are all substitutes for the hard to bare feelings of survival
When you were young you were asked to choose
Between a frog jumping—or its rumble
Of course you picked the lovely splash
Now you think about things from the inside out
And realize it is the enduring noise that is unexpectedly delightful
Just like an honest rejection or a made-up word so you can tame the light

You get rid of the bodies—drinking sherry in your shed
Using a stone to weigh the pages of your life
And stop the ghosts that haunt your bloated heart
Bitter pollen leaves tracks on your blouse
And the brass fanfare tumbles you back
To another march down a long aisle
Flowers lying like sleeping children in your arms
Sprinkling freckles on your knickerbocker glory dress
But at least then the sneezes sounded like cheers
As you walked into the yellow light

Let's Have a Jar*

We have become this unsafe clump / jarred raw and only half-stuffed / our plots fill thimbles / we balance them on narrow fingers / let plans sour on our stoppered tongues / as we're wrung out / / let's pretend we are old / our pink gin schemes jam-packed in a jar / unscrew the lid / taste the preserved possibilities / hold them in your mouth / honey-dipped dates / pickled promises / dropped notes of a complicated concerto / jarring like the idea of spring onions / or writing tears / but a fabulous yawp nonetheless

Jar (informal British English): a glass of beer

ACKNOWLEDGMENTS

Thank you to the following publications, where versions of these poems first appeared, some with different titles:

Bee House Journal "Skewwiff"
Boats Against the Current "March"
Eclectica Magazine "Lines"
The Fib Review "The Fibs We Tell"
Free Flash Fiction "Maybe I Give A Damn"
Hags On Fire "Beyond The Belief Of Selkies"
High Shelf Press "brink"
Hole in the Head Review "Illusions Of A Starry Night" and "Air Turbulence In Small Spaces"
Monday Night Lit "Brown Rapping"
Proverse Press "Daisy in Chains"
Réapparition Journal "Mulling Over First Love"
River Bend Bookshop Press "A Romance Without Comedy"
Sad Girls Club Lit "Passive: Aggressive"
Selcouth Station Press "Relax—Don't Do It"
Shot Glass Review "Interdependence"
Sledgehammer Lit "Let's have A Jar"
Sparked Lit Mag "Splash, A Retrospective"
Tofu Ink Arts Press "Gifts to a Young Lady" and "A Guide to Flash-In-The-Pan Living"
Roi Fainéant Press "Watching Dr Zhivago with my Sister"

Adele Evershed is an educator and writer. She was born in Wales and has lived in Hong Kong and Singapore before settling in Connecticut with her family. Adele started writing in 2019 and since that time her poetry and prose have been published in over seventy online journals such as Every Day Fiction, Variety Pack, Grey Sparrow Journal, High Shelf Press, LEON Lit, Prose Online, and *Shot Glass Journal*. She has also had stories and poems published in several print anthologies, such as the award-winning *81 Words* published by Victorina Press and *A470, Poems for the Road* published by Arachne Press.

She has recently been nominated for The Pushcart Prize for poetry, shortlisted for the Staunch Prize for flash fiction, and her novella in flash, *The History of Hand Thrown Walls*, was shortlisted for the Reflex Press Novella Award. Adele's first poetry chapbook, *Turbulence in Small Spaces*, will be published next year. Read more of her work at thelithag.com

Milton Keynes UK
Ingram Content Group UK Ltd.
UKHW040635301023
431584UK00004B/349